Miracles
of God

Christmas, 2021

Dear Mark & Lisa,

Praying our Lord will bless you both with overflowing love, joy & Peace this Christmas as we celebrate the birth of our Savior! Emmanuel, God with us! You are a wonderful addition to our neighborhood! Our love to you & Family

I will give thanks unto Thee, O Lord, with my whole heart.
I will speak of all Thy marvelous works.
I will be glad and rejoice in Thee:
Yea, my songs will I make of Thy Name, O Thou most highest

Psalm 9: 1-2, Prayer Book Version
The Great Bible (Miles Coverdale, 1488-1569)

Miracles of God

Poems of a Pilgrim

Emily Persons McElhaney

Emily Persons McElhaney

©2015 Emily Persons McElhaney

All rights reserved. No parts of this book may be reproduced or transmitted in any form or by any means, electronic, mechanical, or otherwise without written permission from the author.

ISBN: 978-1-6311-1031-3

Cover Design: BAM! Publishing
Cover Photo: Public Domain

Unless otherwise noted, Scripture quotations taken from the New King James Version®. Copyright © 1982 by Thomas Nelson, Inc. Used by permission. All rights reserved.

Scripture quotations taken from THE AMPLIFIED BIBLE, Copyright © 1954, 1958, 1962, 1964, 1965, 1987 by The Lockman Foundation. All rights reserved. Used by permission. (www.Lockman.org).

Scripture quotations marked NLT are taken from the *Holy Bible*, New Living Translation, copyright © 1996, 2004, 2007, 2013 by Tyndale House Foundation. Used by permission of Tyndale House Publishers Inc., Carol Stream, Illinois 60188. All rights reserved.

The WellHouse logo and "a place of grace" trade marked slogan used by permission of The WellHouse, Leeds, AL 35094. All rights reserved.

Additional copies are made available through:

BAM! Publishing/Espresso Book Machine
Books-A-Million, Brookwood Village
Birmingham, AL 35209
1-205-870-0213
publishing-birmingham@booksamillion.com

Alo available at: www.booksamillion.com/bamauthors

For more information about BAM! Publishing please visit our website
www.bampublish.com

Printed in the United States of America

This book is dedicated to The WellHouse, a ministry that rescues young girls and women from the horrors of human trafficking.

a place of grace.

All proceeds of this book will be donated by the author to The WellHouse in Birmingham, AL.

THE-WELLHOUSE.ORG

Ackowledgements

I am so grateful to Marilyn Cook for the many hours she spent typing my poems, helping me proof them, and getting them ready for print. Thank you, dear Marilyn. Without you this book would not have happened! I pray that God will pour out His love, His peace, His joy and sweetest blessings upon you and your beloved family.

I also want to thank Zach Kendrick at Books-A-Million, Brookwood Village in Birmingham. He is the Espresso Book Machine Operator for the store's BAM! Publishing service. Zach is such an encourager and patiently guided me in selecting my book cover, interior layout, and answering all of my, and Marilyn's, many questions. He is a tremendous asset to Books-A-Million!

TABLE OF CONTENTS

AUTHOR'S NOTE

I accepted Christ as my Savior in my mid-teens and my life, increasingly, centered around Church and its activities. There I met my future husband and we were married in 1956. Although life was good and we were so blessed with Christian friends and were busy serving in our Church, I began to hunger and thirst for a deeper walk with the One I had confessed to be Savior and Lord of my life. I now know that this came from God, Himself, as did my salvation.

About this time, the Lord led us to Cottage Hill Baptist Church in Mobile, Alabama, with a dynamic young pastor, Fred Wolfe. Our pastor not only taught us the deep truths I had been searching for, but he also brought to our church wonderful Bible teachers from all over the world! The Word of God that flowed from their innermost beings was Spirit-anointed, indeed "rivers of Living Water" as Jesus promised in John 7:38. As Psalm 119:130 states, "The entrance of your words gives light, it gives understanding to the simple." And how God's blessed word filled my simple, needy heart with joy overflowing!

I began to hear of a "Quiet Time", a time set aside to spend with our Lord in His Word, meditation and prayer. Luke 10:38-42, is the account of Jesus visiting in the home of Martha and Mary. Martha immediately went to the kitchen and began to busily prepare a meal for her honored Guest, but Mary seated herself at her Lord's feet. In an attitude of worship and with an uncluttered open mind, Mary listened to all her Lord had to say. I was so much like Martha but I longed to be like Mary, to set aside a quiet time with Jesus and "hear" Him speak to me from His Word.

As my own "Quiet Time" began to develop with reading God's Word, meditating on what my Lord had to say to me, personally, and praying, it quickly became the center and focus of my life. I found Psalm 16:11 to be abundantly true: "You will show me the path of life; in Your Presence is fullness of joy, at Your right hand there are pleasures forevermore." Many years ago, I found a poem which I copied and taped in the front of my Bible. Over the years, I have found its words to be abundantly true!

MY BIBLE AND I

We've traveled together, my Bible and I,
Through all kinds of weather, with smile or with sigh;
In sorrow or sunshine, in tempest or calm,
Thy friendship's unchanging, my lamp and my psalm.

We've traveled together, my Bible and I.
When life has grown weary and death e'en was nigh;
But all through the darkness of mist and of wrong,
I found Thee a solace, a prayer or a song.

So, now, who shall part us, my Bible and I?
Shall ism or chism, or new lights who try?
Shall shadow for substance, or stone for good bread,
Supplant its sound wisdom, give folly instead?

Ah, no my dear Bible, revealer of light,
Thou sword of the Spirit, put error to flight!
And still through life's journey, until the last sigh,
We'll travel together, my Bible and I.
Author Unknown

In this book, I have included my own poems expressing the truths God has taught, and is ever teaching, me from His inerrant Word. In sharing these poems, it is my prayer that others, especially beloved family and friends, will seek their own personal relationship and Quiet Time with Christ if they have not already done so.

To my dear children, grandchildren, great-grandchildren and all my generations to come by birth, by marriage or by adoption, I desire to leave a spiritual legacy of faith. A statement Patrick Henry, one of America's greatest patriots, included in his will describes perfectly the deepest longing of my heart for my loved ones:

"I have now disposed of all my property to my family. There is one thing more I wish to give them, and that is faith in Jesus Christ. If they had that and I had not given them one shilling, they would be rich; and if I had not given them that, and had given them all the world, they would be poor indeed."

In this increasingly unstable world we live in, God's Word is the only firm foundation to build our lives upon, the only unchanging, absolute truth to guide our paths and give us wisdom in all the issues of life!

Emily Persons McElhaney
June 2015

"Heaven and earth will pass away, but My words will by no means pass away." *Matthew 24:35*

"Above all, you must realize that no prophesy in Scripture ever came from the Prophet's own understanding, or from human initiative. No, those Prophets were moved by the Holy Spirit, and they spoke from God."

2 Peter 1:20, 21 NLT

"For by Him all things were created, that are in Heaven, and that are in earth, or principalities, or powers. All things were created through Him and for Him." *Colossians 1:16*

"Ah, Lord God! Behold, You have made the heavens and the earth by Your great power and outstretched arm. There is nothing too hard for You." *Jeremiah 32:17*

THE MIRACLES OF GOD

The miracles of God abound
In every atom that is found,
In every cry of newborn babe,
'Til every sigh be hid by spade.

All things appeared from Wisdom's source,
No thing untouched by His great force.
God spoke to ears as yet unformed
And promised life to men unborn.

Within each part of His creation,
God set a seed of procreation.
Foretelling life from start to end,
Confirms the end as it begins.

His flowers flood aesthetic sight
In potpourri of colors bright;
Creation's chorus ever singing
The glorious message of His Being.

1

So deaf can see, the blind can hear,
The mute can feel that God is near.
And souls cast down in deepest sorrow
Can know the sun will rise tomorrow.

For God rides on the wings of wind
To comfort man, his needs attend;
In every rustle of the wind,
From earth to sky and back again.

White clouds form artworks in the sky,
Then banking high they weep and cry.
Their tears fall down to wash the earth;
They disappear and seed gives birth.

From this great reservoir of tears,
Life yet evolves throughout the years,
For nature stands not on its own,
Obeys the One by which it's sown.

The seas appeared, made by His hand,
They keep their bounds at His command.
And hidden there beneath their depths,
His miracles of life and wealth.

God planned the sea as it should be,
In mighty wave, from deepest sea.
Comes yet again and gives the more,
Spills out its treasures on the shore.

He causes night to know its place,
From heaven's womb the morning breaks.
And from its birth begets the dew
To clothe the grass, with strength renew.

The sun He set in its own place,
The moon was gifted by His grace.
The greater and the lesser light
Are miracles of His great might.

Each light of day, each star-filled night
Are evidence of His great might.
Of this most awesome heavenly host,
Not man, but God alone can boast!

He spoke and life appeared on earth,
He marks each one as it gives birth.
All creatures whether great or small
Appear in answer to His call.

In pride of lion, in song of bird,
His miracles are seen and heard.
The mighty ox, the gentle dove
Are miracles of His great love.

From heaven's store the snows fall down,
Like sparkling diamonds on the ground.
Each flake He calls by its own name;
Not one alike, but yet the same.

The trees with leaves of varied splendor
Are loaned by Him, the Holy Lender.
Bowed down with fruit or blessed shade,
Their boughs reach up to Him in praise.

We see the crown of God's creation
In every tribe and tongue and nation.
His miracles He longs to show,
To each His blessings to bestow.

Though some deny our God exists,
In Him alone all things consist.
They walk upon the paths He laid
And speak with tongues that He has made.

If stubborn man would only heed
God's miracles he, too, could see.
What blissful rest and peace of mind
His needy soul would surely find.

For Christ, in deepest agony,
Died on the cross for all to see.
He opened up the way of life
To end in man all fear, all strife.

Oh, God of miracles and might,
Please draw man's soul from earth's dark night.
Through sacrifice of your dear Son,
Impress on man his victory's won!

When man in darkness, bowed 'neath grief,
Seeks not his will to bring relief,
But looks to God as does creation,
Then peace shall come to every nation.

For earth is but a dot in space,
Held tight in time by God's great grace.
And He, alone, holds time's demise;
His will, His plan will come to pass.

The microscopic world within
Of unseen things He did begin.
In myriads of things unknown,
His miracles will yet be shown.

From twinkling stars to sun so bright,
His truth springs forth in floods of light.
Upon a universe so vast,
The miracles of God are cast!

"…The Lord made Heaven and the earth, the sea,
and all that is in them."

Exodus 10:11

"For He spoke, and it was done; He commanded
and it stood fast."

Psalm 33:9

"The earth is the Lord's and everything in it. The world and all its people belong to Him. For He laid the earth's foundation on the seas and built it on the ocean depths."

Psalm 24:1, 2 NLT

"By faith we understand that the worlds were framed by the Word of God, so that the things which are seen were not made of things which are visible."

Hebrews 11:3

"…For what is your life? It is even a vapor that appears for a little time and then vanishes away."
James 4:14

"But the path of the just is like the shining sun, That shines ever brighter unto the perfect day."
Proverbs 4:18

Just For a Little While…

Just for a little while…
This life with all its problems,
For soon our reigning King will come
And by His power will solve them.

Just for a little while…
Our trials, griefs, and sorrows,
For when He comes He'll dry our tears;
Perhaps He'll come tomorrow!

Just for a little while…
Our Savior bids us pray,
And trust His word to guide our steps,
His lamp to light our way.

Just for a little while…
To tell the world of Christ,
Who paid sin's debt for everyone,
God's perfect Sacrifice!

"And Jesus answered and said to her, Martha, Martha, you are worried and troubled about many things. But one thing is needed, and Mary has chosen that good part, which will not be taken away from her." *Luke 10:41*

A MARY I WOULD BE

I've always been a Martha, Lord,
So busy in my work.
Each job I sought to do for You,
No duty did I shirk!

I had no time to spend with You,
I'd other things to do.
I had to go and feed the poor;
Such needs to fill I knew!

My values were all turned around,
Though good works I must do.
I did not know, as Paul of old,
I must first learn of You.

I want to be a Mary, Lord,
And sit at your dear feet.
I want to love and worship You,
Each day with you to meet.

I seek your knowledge as pure gold,
Your word my hidden treasure.
Instruct me in the narrow way,
Your will, my greatest pleasure!

I know not how you'll use me, Lord,
I'll place that in Your care.
I only want to praise You now
And seek Your face so fair.

I will to yield each day to You,
No part would I withhold,
That I may be conformed to You
And come forth as pure gold.

To gaze upon You, dearest Lord,
Though on this earth I stay,
To be as one with You, my Lord,
To walk the light-filled way.

A Mary I would be to You
And stay close by Your side;
My mind and heart Your temple,
Your Spirit now my Guide.

To abide within Your body,
A wild branch grafted in,
To draw from You, most holy Vine,
My life, O dearest Kin.

"But He was wounded for our transgressions, He was bruised for our iniquities; the chastisement for our peace was upon Him, and by His stripes we are healed." *Isaiah 53:5*

"I am the living bread which came down from heaven. If anyone eats of this bread, he will live forever.." *John 6:51a*

HE

He, Who was kindest,
Gave Himself for me.
I, who was blindest,
This Kindest made see.

He, Who was wisest,
All knowledge and learning;
I, who was lacking,
In Him made discerning.

He, the great Shepherd,
Gave Himself for me.
I, the sin-bound one,
This Shepherd set free!

He, the Creator,
Became Son of Man.
I, dead in sin,
In Him born again.

He, the most lovely,
Became the unlovely.
I, the most ugly,
Made lovely in He.

He, all sufficient,
For me became Bread.
I, of lean stature,
To Fullness was led.

"Therefore, if anyone is in Christ, he is a new creation; old things have passed away; behold, all things have become new…Therefore, we are ambassadors for Christ, as though God were pleading through us: we implore you on Christ's behalf, be reconciled to God…For He made Him who knew no sin to be sin for us, that we might become the righteousness of God in Him."

2 Corinthians 5: 17, 20, 21

"But this Man, after He had offered one sacrifice for sins forever, sat down at the right hand of God." *Hebrews 10:12*

HE IS LORD!

Jesus...
Came to seek and save the lost,
He alone could pay the cost,
He, the Son, whom God loved most,
...for He was Lord.

Born to die that we might live,
Messiah came, but He was killed,
Holy Scripture thus fulfilled,
...for He was Lord.

Paid a debt He did not owe,
For the sins He did not sow,
For a world that did not know,
...that He was Lord.

Did a work that is complete,
He'll need never to repeat,
At God's right hand He took His seat,
...for He was Lord.

Hid in Christ to God we're known,
One day soon He'll claim His throne,
We'll rule with Him, for'er His own,
...for He is Lord!

*"For the Son of Man has come to seek
and to save that which was lost."*

Luke 19:10

"…Christ in you, the hope of glory." *Colossians 1:27*

"Let us therefore come boldly to the throne of grace, that we may obtain mercy and find grace to help in time of need." *Hebrews 4:16*

COULD I DOUBT?

Could I doubt a loving Savior,
Could I doubt my soul's best Friend,
Could I doubt He has redeemed me,
Doubt the Holy veil did rend?

Oh, to doubt Him all sufficient
Is to doubt the light of day,
Doubt the sun in glorious rising,
Dressing earth in Heaven's array!

Could I doubt in time of trouble,
Could I doubt in deepest night,
Could I doubt Thy safe pavilion,
Doubt Thee, Master, Source of light?

Oh, to doubt Thy strength and power
Is to put self in Thy place;
Doubt Thee God, great God of mercy,
Source of never-ending grace.

Could I strive with God, my Maker,
Could I say, "Behold! The clay?"
Could I doubt His plan is perfect,
Doubt He keeps earth in His way?

Oh, to doubt so great redemption
Is to shame His precious name,
Doubt He bore my sins on Calvary,
On Himself placed all my shame.

Could I doubt the Mighty Counselor,
Could I doubt the Prince of Peace,
Could I doubt He laid His life down,
Doubt He paid for sin's release?

Oh, to doubt this wondrous Jesus
Is to doubt creation's story,
Doubt He spoke it into being;
Christ, my only hope of glory!

"I have come as a Light into the world, that whoever believes in Me should not abide in darkness." *John 12:46*

"Most assuredly, I say to you, unless a grain of wheat falls into the ground and dies, it remains alone; but if it dies, it produces much grain." *John 12:24*

The Planting of Light

Blessed Light, so pure and shining,
Giving life to all who come;
Holy Seed came down from heaven
For the life of all mankind.

For the plowing up of sorrow
And the planting of the Light,
Will go down into the darkness
Setting tortured captives free.

And Light once entered ne'er departs,
But grows the plant and multiplies,
Giving life and love and mercy
To each hungry, desperate soul.

Who, receiving, satisfied beyond
All measure and delight,
Becomes a sower in the darkness
As the Light bids it to plow.

Such a harvest e'er repeated
Brings the Master fullest yield,
As His plows of love and mercy
Plant the Seed of Light and Life.

Love and mercy are the muscle
Of the soul-life hid in Light;
Life from death and Light from darkness
Breaking forth in victory!

Choosing death, but never dying,
For the Light can never dim;
Growing brighter in the giving
Of its selfless radiance.

For in losing is the gaining
And in giving is the living,
Of the life of love and mercy
Which the darkness cannot know.

Blessed resurrection when
The Light consumes the night,
When defeat gives place to victory
And death gives place to life.

Bringing joy to fields of sorrow,
Joining souls to Christ, the Light,
Christ, the Source of love and mercy,
Never-ending Source of Life!

"How greatly and gradually souls are led into the Kingdom of God. We must prepare the ground. Love is the plough, but the Lord calls us to be the servant 'working the plough' and breaking up the hard ground into which His seed of life is placed. Seed will not grow in hard ground."

Author Unknown

"For God so greatly loved and dearly prized the world that He [even] gave up His only begotten (unique) Son, so that whoever believes in (trusts in, clings to, relies on) Him shall not perish (come to destruction, be lost) but have eternal (everlasting) life."

John 3:16, Amplified Bible

"And He said to me, My grace is sufficient for you, for My strength is made perfect in weakness. Therefore most gladly I will rather boast in my infirmities, that the power of Christ may rest upon me." *2 Corinthians 12:9*

JESUS, JESUS, ALL TO ME

You are all to me, my Jesus:
Master, Lord, my soul's dear Lover,
Comrade, Captain, Father, Mother,
Loving Savior, eldest Brother.

All that beauty is You are,
Morning's Light, yet evening's Star;
Fragrance of the fairest flower,
Cleansing of the springtime shower.

Glory of the radiant sunset,
Victor of the daybreak's conquest.
All that's good You are and more,
Nothing lacking in Your store.

In my inner-man be King,
Ever to You, Lord, I cling.
My will, my heart I give to Thee,
Jesus, Jesus, all to me.

Source of every wind that blows,
Increase of each seed that grows.
Nature subject to Your will,
You speak! At once the storm is still!

No strain too big for Your great power,
Regardless of the day or hour.
You neither slumber, nor yet sleep;
No path I take for You too steep.

My smallest fear or greatest foe,
Severest wound or deepest woe;
My soul cries out to You appealing,
And with Your touch comes peace and healing.

Light of life and Life of light,
Illuminating darkest night.
No power so strong compares to Thee,
Jesus, Jesus, all to me!

"You will keep him in perfect peace, whose mind
is stayed on You, because He trusts in You."
Isaiah 26:3

"Looking unto Jesus, the Author and Finisher of
our faith…" *Hebrews 12:2a*

THE CHRIST, MY SOUL'S GREAT QUEST!

My times are in the hands of Christ
And surely that is best.
There is no other way so sure,
In Him, alone, I'm blest!

Though riches cease or ill winds blow,
Though faith is put to test,
I'll trust in Him for peace and hope;
The Christ, my soul's great Quest!

When mercy His great love withholds,
It's for my good I reason.
When darkness seeks to hide His face,
It's only for a season!

My heart in turmoil looks to Him,
My doubt leans on His breast;
My soul waits only for my Lord,
The Christ, my soul's great Quest!

"The heavens declare the glory of God; and the firmament shows His handiwork." *Psalm 19:1*

"Then God saw everything that He had made, and indeed it was very good. So the evening and the morning were the sixth day.." *Genesis 1:31a*

OH HOW I LOVE A SUMMER DAY

Oh how I love a summer day,
A gentle, lovely time,
With fluffy clouds so downy soft,
To dream a dream sublime:

The mountains' high majestic peaks,
The valleys intervening,
Are laced about by streams so bold,
So constantly careening.

Down the mountain, in the valley,
Flowers are ablooming,
Bees are busy buzzing
From the nectar they're consuming.

The cooling breeze glides through the trees,
A gentle rustling sound,
Then lifting high, it meets the sky
And chases clouds around.

Oh how I love a summer day,
That God alone provides,
If my arms were big enough
I'd fold it all inside!

On the hill, in beauty still,
Are multitudes of flowers,
Where in the fall the goldenrod
Will build its gleaming towers.

The morning glory awakens,
Refreshed in brilliant blue,
While in the vale the violet shy
Still drinks its morning dew.

In my thoughts I pluck the flowers,
Massed in gay profusion,
And rearrange them to create
A rainbow of illusion.

Oh how I love a summer day,
Its beauty fills my being.
The wonders that each day will bring,
I'm thankful just for seeing!

The birds rise up in splendid flight,
Stretching sturdy wing,
And praise the beauty of the earth
With each song they sing.

The butterflies are fluttering
In colors wild and sweet;
So fragile, yet so full of life,
They kiss each flower they meet.

Busy little animals
All scurry from their den,
To work and play before the day,
When summer's glow will end.

Oh how I love a summer day,
The brightest time of all!
It sings to me God's love song
And I beckon to His call.

The busy brook cuts through the meadow,
Singing out its song,
Splishing, splashing, ever dashing
Rock and rolling stone.

But more than merriment is hid,
In waters clear and cold,
The little brook is spreading life
To all it may enfold.

Refreshing joy to weary hearts,
A sparkling brook can bring;
We thank You, Father, for this gift
That from Your riches spring!

Oh how I love a summer day,
God's beauty all around;
Be still dear friend and listen,
For His Presence can be found.

As time goes by and years roll on,
My sight will dim I know,
But inwardly, my memory
Will bring back summer's glow.

I'll view the beauty of God's hand,
I'll hear the bluebirds sing,
I'll dance among the flowers
My sweet memories will bring.

For memories can hold so much,
And mine are busy filling,
Full of happy, joy-filled days
My Father is unreeling.

Oh how I love a summer day,
In dreams all gold and green,
God's creation so infilling,
In a never-ending scene!

*"The entrance of Your words gives light;
it gives understanding to the simple."*

Psalm 119:130

"In the year that King Uzziah died, I saw the Lord sitting on a throne, high and lifted up, and the train of His robe filled the Temple." *Isaiah 6:1*

"They shall see His face, and His name shall be on their foreheads..." *Revelation 22:4*

I HAVE SEEN THE LORD!

I have seen the Lord!
Oh, He is awesome to behold;
Of His beauty and His wonder,
The half has not been told!

I have seen the Lord!
And in love He looked upon me.
He touched my blinded eyes
And now, by grace His truth I see.

I have seen the Lord!
And His mercy healed my soul.
He filled my needy heart with joy,
With richest truth untold.

I have seen the Lord!
And my joy now knows no bounds.
He assured me that his love will e'er
Encircle me around.

I have seen the Lord!
All too glorious in light;
A light that fills creation
With His power and His might.

I have seen the Lord!
And He is lifted up on high.
His mighty ears are open,
To hear my faintest cry.

I have seen the Lord!
Upon my wounded soul He breathed,
As in love I fell before Him,
His Holy Spirit I received.

I have seen the Lord!
Oh, how my heart is filled with song.
From glory unto glory,
His blessed Spirit guides me on.

I have seen the Lord!
Now His forever I will be.
Each day I'll hear Him say these words,
"My child, come sit with Me."

*Certainly, I have not seen the Lord
with my physical eyes! I have seen
the Lord in His beautiful creation, His
blessed word and in my spirit as I have
worshipped Him. One day I will see
my beloved Lord "face to face", as the
lovely old hymn states. We have this
promise in I John 3:2 "…we know that
when He is revealed, we shall be like
Him, for we shall see Him as He is."*

"Let my mouth be filled with Your praise and with Your glory all the day." *Psalm 71:8*

I Praise Thee, Father, Lord of All

I praise Thee, Father, Lord of all,
With loving heart and listening ear,
With yielded hand and moving feet
I listen, Lord, I hear, I hear.

I praise Thee, Father, Lord of all,
In yieldedness, on bended knee.
Teach me Thy way, Oh Lord my God,
So that in part, I see, I see.

I praise Thee, Father, Lord of all,
With gratefulness Thy praise bestow.
Implant in me Thy seed of life
And then my Lord, I'll grow, I'll grow.

I praise Thee, Father, Lord of all,
I read Thy word expectantly!
Thy Holy Spirit fills my soul,
Reveals thy word to me, to me.

I praise Thee, Father, Lord of all,
Instill in me Thy will to know,
When Your sweet Spirit says to me,
"My sheep are lost", I'll go, I'll go.

"When You said, 'Seek My face', my heart said to You, 'Your face, Lord, I will seek'." *Psalm 27:8*

IN HIS PRESENCE

Time alone with Him,
My blessed King,
Makes my heart, my soul
With praises sing.

His presence ever sought,
Yet seeking still,
The wonder of His love
My heart to fill.

In worship, there, I gaze
On His dear face.
My worldly woes and cares
He does erase.

No place is more secure
When hid in Christ,
For He is God Himself
Who gives me life.

And in His Presence safe
I trust and rest;
His power knows no end
And I am blessed.

As Amy Carmichael states in her little book, *Edges of His Ways*[1], "What does this or that matter when He is in control." My faithful Father and my King, Jesus Christ, is working all things together for His glory and my eternal good.

[1] Amy Carmichael *Edges of His Ways*. CLC Publications, Fort Washington, PA. 1980.

"And so, dear brothers and sisters, I plead with you to give your bodies to God because of all He has done for you. Let them be a living and holy sacrifice – the kind He will find acceptable. This is truly the way to worship Him. Don't copy the behavior and customs of this world, but let God transform you into a new person by changing the way you think. Then you will learn to know God's will for you, which is good and pleasing and perfect."

Romans 12: 1,2 NLT

"This is a faithful saying and worthy of all acceptance, that Christ Jesus came into the world to save sinners, of whom I am chief." *I Timothy 1:15*

WHO ELSE BUT HE, MY JESUS

Who else but He, my Jesus,
Could love one such as I,
And look beyond my fearful heart
To hear my inner cry.

Who else but He could feel the pain
Of cruel separation,
And reconcile me back to God
By His death and reparation.

Who else but He, my Jesus,
Could change the course of man,
O'ercome the lies of Satan
And destroy the root of sin.

Who else but He could take a life
So filled with imperfection,
And change it into love so rich,
To live in His reflection.

That one was I, so mean and crude,
So filled with pride and self;
He birthed me, yea, now prunes me,
'Til He is all that's left.

"But now, O Lord, You are our Father; we are the clay, and You our Potter; and all we are the work of Your Hand." *Isaiah 64:8*

THE MASTER POTTER

Oh Jesus, take this stubborn clay
And fashion me again.
Make me a vessel clean and pure
With Thy great Potter's hand.

For in Thy hands I'm ever safe,
There's naught to fear from Thee;
Thou art the Master Potter
With a special plan for me.

Please take Your knife, dear Potter,
Probe deep within my heart,
Cut out the lumps of stubborn clay;
O spare not any part!

Apply the water of Thy word,
To soften my hard heart,
That I may yield to Thy sweet touch,
Renewed in every part.

A vessel unto honor,
Shaped by Thy loving hand,
Then fill me up and pour me out
To serve Thy master-plan.

"...I have come that they may have life, and that they may have it more abundantly." *John 10:10b*

"Jesus said to him, I am the Way, the Truth, and the Life. No one comes to the Father except through Me." *John 14:6*

The Greatest Miracle

Has Jesus ever said to you
Those most glorious of words,
An invitation to your heart,
Most precious ever heard?

"Oh come and see the place I am,
Oh come and dwell with Me.
Great peace and joy I'll give to you,
Such gifts I give are free."

My Lord, this greatest miracle
Occurred in me one day.
You took my wretched, sinful life
Pointing me into Your Way.

The greatest miracle of all,
A life that's been set free;
Transformed into Your Image
Throughout Eternity.

"I will go before you, and make the crooked places straight; I will break in pieces the gates of bronze and cut the bars of iron. I will give you the treasures of darkness and hidden riches of secret places..."

Isaiah 45:2,3a

"Who among you that fears the Lord? Who obeys the voices of His servant? Who walks in darkness and has no light? Let him trust in the name of the Lord and rely upon his God."
Isaiah 50:10

"Be of good courage, And He shall strengthen your heart, All you who hope in the Lord."
Psalm 31:24

THE WINTER OF MY HEART

My heart is filled with winter's icy breath,
A valley of the deepest, darkest night.
For sorrow and despair companion there,
To shut out heaven's joy and radiant light.

Yet even here, a place of ill delight,
My heart is fixed on Christ, my reigning King.
Beloved of all loves, desiring still,
His praise and wondrous majesty to sing.

I yet know, within my inmost being,
My Lord still rules, in victory enthroned.
And though the wicked one oppress me sore,
The time will come when Christ will right each wrong.

This wintry ice will melt away, o'ercome,
By warmth from faithful spring's sweet breath.
God's might and strength will break these icy bonds
And life spring forth from winter's bed of death.

This valley shadowed all around with fears,
Will burst forth singing in that blessed hour.
The chilling winds of winter will abate,
Surrendered to the Lord and His great power!

The winter of my heart will flee away,
As Christ shines forth His love so radiantly,
And this poor, needy one will leap for joy,
When present hope becomes reality!

A.W. Tozer said, "Seldom does God use one whom He has not hurt deeply. As objects of God's great love, we should welcome trouble as friends."

"The heart that yet can hope and trust,
and cry to Thee though from the dust,
Is all unconquered still."
By Paul Gerhardt

"Do not rejoice over me, my enemy; when I fall, I will arise; when I sit in darkness, the Lord will be a Light to me."

Micah 7:8

"Abide in Me, and I in you. As the branch cannot bear fruit of itself, unless it abides in the vine, neither can you, unless you abide in Me." *John 15:4*

"I will praise You, O Lord, with my whole heart; I will tell of all Your marvelous works." *Psalm 9:1*

ABIDING IN HIS PRESENCE

Abandoning my life to Jesus,
Loving, serving as He calls.
Streams of mercy overflowing,
As I yield to Him my all.

Flow through me, O Living Water,
Let God's love to others flow.
Seeing only in me Jesus,
As His life implanted grows.

All my sin placed on my Savior,
Washed me whiter than the snow,
Dressed me in the finest linen;
Like Him, Father, may I grow.

Bringing all my thoughts to Jesus,
Though my faith be tiny seed;
Counting all things joy and gladness,
Be it plenty, be it need.

When the gloom seeks to enclose me,
Rise my heart alone to be,
Abiding ever in His Presence,
Victory assured, indeed!

I will lift my eyes to Jesus,
Ever present help in need.
Finding Him, the All-Sufficient,
Source of mercy, grace indeed!

'Til by faith, He calls me homeward,
My heart sings to Him my love.
'Til my song is then perfected,
As I dwell with Him above.

Then from glory unto glory,
Drawing from Him life so sweet,
Abiding ever in His Presence,
Throughout all eternity!

"For the Lord Himself will descend from heaven with a shout, and the voice of an archangel, and with the trumpet of God. And the dead in Christ will rise first. Then we who are alive and remain shall be caught up together with them in the clouds to meet the Lord in the air. And thus we shall always be with the Lord." *I Thessalonians 4:16,17*

If God Be For Us...

Oh God, may we in Your great strength brave be,
With eyes and wills, like flint, set only upon Thee.
Though battles rage, in Thee alone we trust!
Still, through them all, Thy truth shall lead us...thus:
"If God be for us, who can be against us!"

When trumpets sound upon that last great day,
And all your soldiers meet in white array,
Amazed, we'll look on earthly scene below
And see, for'er defeated, our great foe!
"If God be for us, who can be against us!"

Until we hear the angel's shout, "You're free!"
"Arise, come forth, thy Bridegroom calls for thee,"
Surrounded by thy might and armor strong,
We fight, we march to that great, gladsome song:
"If God be for us, who can be against us!"

"Remember the things I have done in the past. For I alone am God! I am God, and there is none like Me. Only I can tell you the future before it even happens. Everything I plan will come to pass, for I do whatever I wish."

Isaiah 46:9,10 NLT

"Behold children are a heritage from the Lord, the fruit of the womb is a reward." *Psalm 127:3*

"Train up a child in the way he should go,
And when he is old he will not depart from it."
Proverbs 22:6

Precious Little Hands of Love

One day, my dearest children,
You brought to me a treasure;
The imprint of your little hands,
A gift beyond all measure!

I placed them high upon my wall,
Where all throughout the day,
I'd look and see those little hands
And almost hear you say:

"We're this high, Mommy, see how big
We're growing every day!"
And then you'd laugh, or skip and jump;
So joyfully you'd play!

Each day I pray, "Lord bless and keep
My children from all wrong.
Implant in them your gift of love,
Your truth to keep them strong."

How quickly years can slip away,
But memories ne'er depart,
For all these precious, childhood days
Are kept within my heart.

Remembering these happy times
Is easy for I'll see,
Your precious little hands of love
Still looking down on me.

"Too much love never spoils children, children become spoiled when we substitute "presents" for presence."

Dr. Anthony P. Witham,
<u>God's Little Devotional Book For Moms</u>[1]

At some point in their childhood, each of my three children brought me the imprint of their hands. Although they are adults now and have families of their own, I still treasure the imprint of their "precious little hands of love"!

[1] *God's Little Devontion Book for Moms*. Honor Books, Colorado Springs, CO. 1995.

"Now this is the confidence that we have in Him, that if we ask anything according to His will, He hears us. And if we know that He hears us, whatever we ask, we know that we have the petitions that we have asked of Him."

I John 5:14, 15

"Believe in the Lord Jesus and you will be saved,
along with everyone in your household."
Acts 16:31 NLT

A Parents' Prayer

*Protect our children, Lord, we pray
And keep them safe by night and day.
Reveal to them the light of Christ;
In sin's dark world, a beacon bright.*

*Show to them, Lord, Thy Holy Son
Whose finished work their victory won.
Set them apart for Jesus' sake;
For their sin, too, His heart did break.*

*A sure foundation Jesus lay,
For our dear children on that day.
From His safe arms no man can steal
Their precious souls or minds to kill.*

*Our God, show them what You require,
That they must first put self to fire.
But from that place of death life comes;
To victory, defeat succumbs!*

*When friends seem far away and few,
Companionship You'll give them, too.
Of Thy great love to them deploy,
That they may sing with sweetest joy!*

Although they seem so all alone,
Within their hearts Thy kingdom's come.
The veil is rent and Christ is there,
To share their every thought and care.

Christ's saving blood o'er them we claim,
That they may never bring Him shame.
Thy perfect plan for them we plead,
Implant in them Thy Holy Seed.

Teach us that we must till the earth,
So that Thy Seed will bring new birth.
Within our homes no fallow ground;
Oh Christ, our King, in them be found!

"Ask God to 'take charge' of your loved ones and to save them at any cost to you or to them. Pray around your loved ones and look to the Lord to control circumstances. Rejoice in the fact that God is working in his or her life – do not look at appearances. Rest in the fact that our omnipotent Lord is working – even when there is no outward evidence. Keep praising the Lord in the darkest hour – and you shall see the desired results. Your loved one will be saved in God's time and on His terms, all for HIS GLORY!"

Morris M. Townsend

"Then the angel said to them, 'Do not be afraid, for behold, I bring you good tidings of great joy which will be to all people. For there is born to you this day in the city of David a Savior, who is Christ the Lord'...Glory to God in the highest, And on earth peace, goodwill toward men!"

Luke 2:10, 14

THAT FIRST GREAT CHRISTMAS MORN

Dearest Babe of Bethlehem,
We worship at Your feet.
We bow before Your manger bed,
To praise You as You sleep.

High above Your precious head,
The angel-host are singing,
"Glory to the newborn King;
Salvation He is bringing!"

The glory that is Yours alone,
You laid aside for man,
And born to us that blessed day
Redemption by Thy hand.

Oh Bethlehem, Thy dearest yield
Was Christ of lowly birth;
Heaven's sweetest essence
Descended down to earth.

God's Word made flesh, His own dear son,
That holy night was born,
And filled the earth with hope and light
That first great Christmas morn!

"And the Word became flesh and dwelt among us,
and we beheld His glory, the glory as of the only
Begotten of the Father, full of grace and truth."
John 1:14

"Remember the things I have done in the past. For I alone am God! I am God, and there is none like Me. Only I can tell you the future before it even happens. Everything I plan will come to pass, for I do whatever I wish."

Isaiah 46:9,10 NLT

"If then you have been raised with Christ [to a new life, thus sharing His resurrection from the dead], aim at and seek the [rich, eternal treasures] that are above, where Christ is, seated at the right hand of God. And set your minds and keep them set on what is above (the higher things), not on the things that are on the earth."
Colossians 3:1,2 Amplified Bible

He Saved Me

Christ took my aimless, shattered life,
Each tiny, broken part,
And in His gentle hands of love
Made me a brand new heart.

When there was none to help me,
He saved me by His grace.
And now, in storm or calmness,
I seek only His dear face.

Such abundance that He gives me,
I scarce can tell you now.
To you, dear friend, He'll give it, too.
Please let me tell you how:

Believe in Christ with all your heart,
Confess to Him your sin.
Invite Him to control your life,
Then surely He'll come in!

In the fullness of His precious Word,
Each day will bring new treasure.
Just keep your eyes on Jesus;
He blesses without measure!

"If we confess our sins, He is faithful and just to forgive us our sins and to cleanse us from all unrighteousness."

I John 1:9

"Eye has not seen, nor ear heard, nor have entered into the heart of man the things which God has prepared for those who love Him. But God has revealed them to us through His Spirit. For the Spirit searches all things, yes, the deep things of God." *I Corinthians 2:9,10*

THE END OF DAY

How I love the end of day,
When the cares of a busy world
Are eased away and I can sit
And contemplate the peacefulness of twilight.

It brushes me with its velvety softness
And I seem to feel the hand of God upon my face.
I reach out to touch and feel His love;
Not with hand but heart.

The brilliant hues of the sunset fill the sky
And the world sits in awesome hush at its grandeur.
It lifts my spirit and I know
I am one with my heavenly Father.

What is this feeling that expands my heart
With a quiet, yet expectant, happiness?
I seem to drink from a golden cup of purest water;
So infilling, without beginning, without ending.

It seems at day's end that I rest,
As if suspended between time and eternity,
And my heart cry echoes
Through the light and swift years of my being.

A being that I know
Has yet to start its fullest life;
A life so rich and sweet that my mortal self
Cannot perceive it. Yet, I long for it!

I wrote the above poem as I sat on the deck of our home on Dauphin Island. That was one of my favorite things to do at my favorite time of day, sunset. What wonderful memories I have of time spent with my Lord and with beloved family and friends at our family home on Dauphin Island, which we named "A Relative Place".

"My sheep hear My voice, and I know them, and they follow Me. And I give them eternal life, and they shall never perish; neither shall anyone snatch them out of My hand. My Father, Who has given them to Me, is greater than all; and no one is able to snatch them out of My Father's hand. I and My Father are One."

John 10:27-30

HOLY LOVE

Oh Holy Love, Thee we adore
And humbly seek to praise Thee more;
In breath, in word, in deed, in song,
Our lives to Thee alone, belong.

Though evil seeks to steal our soul,
We're ever safe within Thy fold.
When darkness comes, in Thee we'll hide
And in Thy Light, we'll e'er reside.

Beneath Your sheltering wings so strong,
We're safe from Satan's demon throng.
Our Holy Priest, turn evil's tide;
In Thee, Beloved, we abide.

We have no need You have not met.
Before our births our paths You set;
To live a life for Thee apart,
To give to You our mind, our heart.

We have no time that is our own,
Our time is Thine and Thine alone.
Thy strength alone to us infill,
To do each moment what you will.

Lord, send Thy holy fire on us,
Consuming greed, all hate, all lust.
Create in us Thy love so pure,
That through the fire will e'er endure.

Oh Holy Love, in purest state,
Conform us to our Holy Mate;
So when He comes to seek His bride,
Prepared we'll rush to His dear side!

"Every Word of God is pure; He is a shield to those who put their trust in Him. Do not add to His words, lest He rebuke you and you be found a liar."

Proverbs 30:5,6

"Then we who are alive and remain shall be caught up together with them in the clouds to meet the Lord in the air. And thus we shall always be with the Lord. Therefore comfort one another with these words." *I Thessalonians 4:17,18*

MY CHILD, WHY DID YOU GO?

Oh child of love, my heart, why did you go?
It seems not long ago God let you grow,
To form so perfect in that inner part,
Then coming forth you claimed this mother's heart.

Travail of pain was only for a while,
For soon I saw your first sweet, tender smile.
I felt your little mouth upon my breast,
To succor you with strength for life's great test.

Where is the child who ran around my knee
And lisped, "Please, mommy, come and play with me!"
Who came to me with all her childlike fear
To comfort, kiss, and wipe away each tear?

The years passed swiftly by like rushing water;
No more my little child, but now my daughter.
Each phase of life you seemed to savor more;
Though problems came, love swept them from our door.

The promise of young womanhood upon you,
A perfect flowering bud 'neath glistening dew,
With beauty soft and lovely hidden there,
Began to burst upon the day so fair.

Just when your future seemed so very bright,
With friends so true and days so filled with light,
You slipped away like twilight's last faint gleam,
Elusive to my hold like some lost dream.

Like sunbeams dancing on a distant wall,
The shadows flee, once more I hear you call.
I reach out eager arms to hold you tight
And, for a moment, end your golden flight.

I now embrace each precious, tender thought,
With mother's love, each sweet remembrance caught.
Imprinting it before the time can sever,
Secure in heart and mind, like you, forever.

But sweetest love, the sun that once was high
Is slipping low beneath a radiant sky!
God's promises, so sure, will soon come true
And Mother, then, will come to be with you!

At the request of a dear friend, Dot Ballard, I wrote the above poem. Dot's thirteen year old daughter and her best friend were on a trip with Dot's parents. A log truck was coming down a hill toward them when it lost control and slammed into their car. The daughter's friend was killed instantly! Dot asked me to write a poem to comfort the grieving mother.

"You thrill me, Lord, with all you have done for me! I sing for joy because of what you have done. Oh, Lord, what great works you do!"

Psalm 92:4,5b NLT

"O Lord, our Lord, How excellent is Your name in all the earth!" *Psalm 8:9*

JESUS

*There is no name
like His dear name,
No greater strength,
nor stronger frame.*

*There is no face
like His dear face.
At His pierced side
I take my place.*

*There is no joy
nor sweeter peace,
That Jesus gives
with sin's release.*

*There is no love
that will compare
To Jesus' love;
He'll ever care.*

There is no path
so straight or true,
So free from worry
He'll give you.

There is no way
For Him too steep;
hinds' feet He'll give
His path to keep.

There is no trial,
however sore,
That He has not
been there before.

There is no sin
He cannot cleanse,
No broken heart
He cannot mend.

There is no life
He has not sought;
With His own blood,
your freedom bought.

There is no hate
He can't resolve,
To deepest love
He'll sure evolve.

There is no friend
so kind as He.
When others stray
He'll stay with thee.

There is no problem
too mundane,
His victory o'er it
to proclaim.

There is no talent,
great or small,
He does not want;
give Him your all!

There is no light
nor radiant glory,
Compared to Christ's
unfolding story.

There is no Priest
like our dear Priest,
At God's right hand
prepares our feast.

There is no other
Mediator,
Than God the Son,
Our Creator.

"And whatever you do in word or deed, do all in the name of the Lord Jesus, giving thanks to God the Father through Him."

Colossians 3:17

LITTLE THINGS

*The little things well done for Christ
Do matter most in life;
A gentle touch, a smile of love
That pleases God above.*

*So often in life's journey,
A heart is bent in sorrow.
A word of cheer can bring them joy
And strength for each tomorrow.*

*So never think the small things,
Of which you never boast,
The little things well done for Christ,
Do matter most in life!*

"Down in the human heart, crushed by the temptor,
Feelings lie buried that grace can restore;
Touched by a loving heart, wakened by kindness,
Chords that are broken will vibrate once more."

Fanny Crosby

"Owe no one anything except to love one another, for he who loves another has fulfilled the law."

Romans 13:8

JUDD AND HIS JEEP

T'was a month before Christmas,
As we both recall,
When we came to Haiti
To visit you all.

We had no idea
What we would find;
Such sights and such sounds
Never entered our minds!

The streets were so crowded,
The traffic so wild;
The drivers would kill you
With nary a smile!

Each morning at dawn
Judd revved up his jeep.
He shouted to all,
"We've got schedules to keep!"

He hopped in his jeep,
To his team gave a whistle,
And away we all flew
Like a yellow-streaked missile!

"On Ethyle, on J.J.,
On Emily and Gwen,
Throughout all of Haiti
We've battles to win!"

Judd and his jeep
Were simply amazing.
He drove through the streets
With his jeep horn ablazing!

We flew round the corners,
Our hearts beating wildly.
Were we a bit scared?
That's putting it mildly!

But Judd was so able
In his yellow jeep;
No road was too rough,
No trail was too steep.

Our trip to Haiti
Won't soon leave our mind,
For Judd and his jeep
Are one of a kind!

By Gwen Reid and Emily McElhaney
Christmas 1990

Gwen and I had gone to Port au Prince, Haiti, to help missionaries, Judd and
Ethyle Williams, with their Christmas outreach.

"Let the word of Christ dwell in you richly in all wisdom, teaching and admonishing one another in psalms and hymns and spiritual songs, singing with grace in your hearts to the Lord."
Colossians 3:16

"Every word of God is pure;
He is a shield to those who put their trust in Him." *Proverbs 30:5*

The Wonders of God's Word

Lord, disentangle all our thoughts,
Enable us to see,
The wonders of Your blessed word,
Now and eternally.

Please give expression to our thoughts
And speak through each to all,
That others, Lord, be brought to Thee
In answer to Your call.

Open wide our hearts, our minds,
Your truth to each be shown.
Your plan to teach, Your love for each,
To trust in Thee alone.

For faith and trust came by Your Word,
Your will for all revealed,
Salvation through Your Holy Son,
No longer, Lord, concealed!

"And my God shall supply all your need according to His riches in glory by Christ Jesus."
Philippians 4:19

"He who believes in Me, as the Scripture has said, out of his heart will flow rivers of living water."
John 7:38

GOD HEARS

Throughout the world of time and space,
God hears our prayer, extends His grace.
It pleases Him to see us bow,
In faith to trust His "why" and "how".

In every need, however small,
In every sigh, He hears our call.
He foreordained in Holy Seed,
To fully meet our every need.

Where thoughts begin, brand us Your own,
With holy fire from Your great throne.
Refill our hearts, so weak and frail,
With fullness from Your Holy Grail.

This fullness that is Living Water,
Came down to save our sons and daughters.
To flow through us throughout our days;
Our God, forever, hear our praise!

"All scripture is inspired by God and is useful to teach us what is true and to make us realize what is wrong in our lives. It corrects us when we are wrong and teaches us to do what is right. God uses it to prepare and equip His people to do every good work."

2 Timothy 3:16,17 NLT

"Hear my cry, O God; attend to my prayer. From the end of the earth I will cry to You, when my heart is overwhelmed; lead me to the Rock that is higher than I". *Psalm 61:1,2*

LORD...HEAR MY CRY

Lord, hear my fervent cry!
I am so blind I cannot see;
Oh, take my hand, lead me to Thee.

Lord, hear my fervent cry!
I am so deaf I cannot hear;
Make me to hear, please draw me near.

Lord, hear my fervent cry!
I am so dumb I cannot speak,
Your perfect peace that all men seek.

Lord, hear my fervent cry!
See through my eyes, hear with my ears,
Speak with my tongue that all may hear.

"I cried out to God with my voice; and He gave ear to my trouble."

Psalm 77:1

"A new commandment I give to you, that you love one another; as I have loved you, that you love one another. By this all will know that you are my disciples, if you have love for one another."
John 13:34, 35

GOD'S LOVE

Oh Love of God, please search and see,
If there be one I do not love.
Oh Light of God, shine down I pray,
Flow Love through me from up above.

On that foundation, Lord, I stand;
Eternal love, my hiding place.
I bow before thy blessed throne;
Oh fill me with Thy love. Make haste!

Such wondrous love has set me free,
And placed me safe on Thee, in Thee.
Unshackled from the world below,
Forever in Your love I'll grow.

Some years ago, my Lord showed me that, too often, I was guilty of a critical spirit toward others. Guarding my mind and heart against this temptation has been so liberating and has freed me up to truly love others, especially those I had exhibited a critical, judgmental spirit toward. The following quote by C.S. Lewis reinforces what our attitude should be toward all others. "To be a Christian means to forgive the inexcusable in others because God has forgiven the inexcusable in you!"

"Do not judge others, and you will not be judged. Do not condemn others, or it will all come back against you. Forgive others, and you will be forgiven.

Luke 6:37 NLT

"All praise to God, the Father of our Lord Jesus Christ. It is by His great mercy that we have been born again, because God raised Jesus Christ from the dead. Now we live with great expectation, and we have a priceless inheritance – an inheritance that is kept in heaven for you, pure and undefiled, beyond the reach of change and decay."

I Peter 1:3,4 NLT

To See With Eyes of Jesus

Oh, to see with eyes of Jesus
As He looks on Heaven's scene.
And to know His peace eternal,
Keeping spirits quiet, serene.

In my thoughts, I climb the stairway
Leading to those courts above,
And my being fills with wonder,
Bursts with ecstasy and love!

He has said man can't imagine
What He has for us up there,
And excitement mounts within me,
As I climb each golden stair.

How the music fills my being
With such rhapsodies of joy,
And the weight of earth is melting
As each care He does destroy.

Streaming tears upon my face
Are turned to crystal iridescent;
Worldly trappings all have vanished,
Fallen as I gain ascent.

Now the gates of splendor open
And I enter into rest.
Holy angels, beauty gleaming,
Lean me safe on Jesus' breast.

Safe am I in my Beloved,
Safe within that holy place.
Hidden truths are now revealed
As I see Jesus face to face!

"How lovely are Your tabernacles, Oh Lord of hosts! My soul yearns, yes, even pines and is homesick for the courts of the Lord; my heart and my flesh cry out and sing for joy to the living God."

Psalm 84:1,2 Amplified Bible

"His eyes were like a flame of fire, and on His head were many crowns. He had a name written that no one knew except Himself. He was clothed with a robe dipped in blood, and His name is called The Word of God."

Revelation 19:12,13

"I am the Alpha and the Omega, the Beginning and the End, says the Lord, who is and who was and who is to come, the Almighty." *Revelation 1:8*

"Looking unto Jesus, the author and finisher of our faith..." *Hebrews 12:2a*

ALPHA AND OMEGA

You are Alpha and Omega,
My beginning and my end.
Abiding ever in Your Being,
Earthly life I'll soon transcend.

Image of my heavenly Father,
Brighter than the brightest light.
Longs my being for Your Presence,
Kept by Your great power and might.

Bowing low my will before you,
Longs my heart to serve, obey.
Committing all my rights to You, Lord,
All I do, in all I say.

You are He who ever was,
Ever is and e'er shall be.
Through the journey of this earth-life,
Longs my heart Your face to see!

"For He Himself has said, 'I will never leave you nor forsake you'."

Hebrews 13:5b

HE WALKS WITH ME

Daily my Lord walks with me,
Drawing me yet higher still,
Nearer to the Christ, my Lord;
Wanting only His dear will.

No good thing my Lord withholds,
Trusting Him in storm or gale,
My heart on Him is ever stayed;
His love for me will never fail!

Each new day, He talks with me.
Carefully, He guards my path,
Sets my feet in His sure steps;
Keeps me safe from Satan's wrath!

He fills my heart with deepest joy,
Even when the sorrows come;
Embraces me with tenderest love,
Assures me that the victory's won.

Each passing day, I love Him more!
Though doubts assail, I'll cling to Christ
And trust Him as His plan unfolds;
In Christ, alone, my hope will last!

"But I am poor and needy; yet the Lord thinks upon me. You are my help and my Deliverer, do not delay, O my God."

Psalm 40:17

I Count Him True

At times, my Lord, I do not see,
I cannot pray, I do not feel.
The darkness hems me all around;
Your joy this evil steals!

As heaviness surrounds my heart
And evil speaks its lies,
And tells me God no longer cares;
His grace to me denies!

I raise my feeble heart to Him,
Who yet sits on His throne,
And think of all His promises
That tell me I'm His own.

By faith refusing fiery darts,
The lies of Satan's wrath;
I count upon God's faithfulness,
His Light to guide my path.

My stubborn will, my feeble faith,
I cast before my King.
By faith, alone, I count Him true,
By faith to Christ I'll cling!

"Let the Word of Christ dwell in you richly in all wisdom, teaching and admonishing one another in psalms and hymns and spiritual songs, singing with grace in your hearts to the Lord."

Colossians 3:16

"For He satisfies the longing soul, and fills the hungry soul with goodness." *Psalm 107:9*

"How sweet are Your words to my taste, Sweeter than honey to my mouth!" *Psalm 119:103*

YOU SATISFY!

My mind, though filled with anxious thoughts,
Looks up to Thee above.
You comprehend my longing heart
And fill me with Your love.

Your Holy Spirit enters in
The borders of my heart,
And fills and floods with perfect peace,
The whole, not just a part!

Each morning as I meet with You,
You fill me with Your bread.
You satisfy my hungry heart;
By your Spirit I am fed.

"Then He spoke a parable to them, that men always ought to pray and not lose heart." *Luke 18:1*

When Saints Pray

Oh, saint, have you a time alone with God,
A time with Him so precious and so dear?
When things of earth just simply fade away,
As you seek the face of God and He draws near?

A time that you can never share with others,
For it is meant, alone, for God's dear pleasure.
A time to kneel before the Throne in Jesus,
To worship and adore Him without measure.

Our wondrous Lord is saddened if we come not,
To fellowship and praise Him every day.
He waits in expectation for our knees to bend,
To turn from cares of life and come His way.

The heavens hush and God bends low His ear,
As we pray and seek His blessed face so fair.
Our Holy Intercessor waits above,
The prayers of saints to mix with incense there.

It matters not if words do not come easy,
For the Holy Spirit groans within our heart,
To show each sin of life we must confess,
To cleanse us and Christ's purity impart.

Oh, none can ever steal us from His hand,
But sin untold will not allow prayer in.
We must seek the laver of His cleansing word,
To wash away the dirt of cancelled sin.

Then clothed in Jesus' righteousness alone,
Our fellowship with Him will grow each day.
Oh, ever seek His blessed Kingdom first,
For wondrous things will happen when saints pray!

The fragrance of our prayers made pure in Jesus
Wafts gently from His Body in that place,
For Christ, in love, made firm our union there;
When He died for sin, God saved us by His grace.

As saints bow low before the Holy One,
Placing songs of praise and adoration there,
The Source of Light that never dims nor fades,
Reflects upon the face of saints in prayer.

"And the Holy Spirit helps us in our weakness. For example, we don't know what God wants us to pray for. But the Holy Spirit prays for us with groanings that cannot be expressed in words. And the Father who knows all hearts knows what the Spirit is saying, for the Spirit pleads for us believers in harmony with God's own will."
Romans 8:26,27 NLT

85

"These things I have spoken to you, that in Me you may have peace. In the world you will have tribulation; but be of good cheer, I have overcome the world." *John 16:33*

"For we walk by faith, not by sight."
2 Corinthians 5:7

ABANDONED IN THE RISEN LORD

No thought of self, most Holy God,
My only need to dwell in Christ.
Abandoned in the risen Lord,
His perfect peace for'er will last.

I do not know what trial may come,
What testing sore, what obstacle.
I only know Christ is my all,
My Guardian from every fall.

I cannot see around the bend
The heartache deep, the sadness there,
But I can see through eyes of faith,
Christ holds me close within His care.

Enveloped in the Christ I love,
It matters not what pain I meet.
Can only come from His dear hand;
In Him all circumstance made sweet!

Christ's ark most holy is my heart;
No man within it can invade.
Bowed down in holy, reverent praise,
This life is e'er before Him laid.

By faith, I now embrace my cross,
As dross of gold consumed by fire;
Made hotter still with each new trial,
But oh what joy, my purifier!

With winged feet and singing heart,
I'll journey through this veil of night;
Abandoned in the risen Lord,
Where thickest dark is brightest light!

"There's nothing about a circumstance that automatically creates anxiety. Anxiety occurs because of the way we respond to a problem or troubling situation. Your ability to choose is part of God's gift of free will to every human being. You can choose how you feel. You can choose what you think about, and you can choose how you will respond to a circumstance."

God's Way Day By Day[1]
Charles Stanley

---

[1] Charles Stanley, *God's Way Day By Day*. Thomas Nelson Publishers, Nashville, TN. 2007.

"Since you have been raised to new life with Christ, set your sights on the realities of heaven, where Christ sits in the place of honor at God's right hand. Think about the things of heaven, not the things of earth. For you died to this life, and your real life is hidden with Christ in God. And when Christ, Who is your life, is revealed to the whole world, you will share in all His glory."

Colossians 3:1-4 NLT

"For He is Lord of lords and King of kings, and those who are with Him are called, chosen, and faithful." *Revelations: 17:14b*

"As for God, His way is perfect; The word of the Lord is proven; He is a shield to all who trust in Him." *Psalm 18:30*

King of Kings, Lord of Lords

Each day I sit with You, my Lord,
The fruit You give so sweet.
It satisfies my deepest need;
Unto my soul as meat.

Your countenance, as purest Light,
Shines down on me, Your own,
Surrounding, filling with Yourself;
I worship You alone.

Hid there within my heart, my mind,
To heed my every call,
Your Spirit strong brings forth Your word;
A ready sword for all.

Oh, be Thou glorified through me,
So all can see, can know,
That you, alone, can set them free;
Your truth within them grow.

You are the Pearl of greatest price,
More worth than all earth's gold;
More fragrant then the sweetest flow'r,
God's Son, so long foretold.

There's none compared to Thy great might,
No beauty like to Thee.
You are the King of kings forever,
Lord of lords to me!

"You will keep him in perfect peace, whose mind is stayed on You, because he trusts in You."
Isaiah 26:3

"I will both lie down in peace, and sleep; For You alone, O Lord, make me dwell in safety." *Psalm 4:8*

In Perfect Peace

This present trial, however hard,
Comes from Your perfect plan,
To cleanse and purify my faith;
A blessing from Your hand!

Your promises I claim my own;
Your angels all about me.
My mouth sings praises to Your Name;
All fears and worries flee!

In perfect peace I lay me down,
To rest in Your dear hand.
You fill my heart, it overflows
With joy at Your command!

"For no temptation (no trial regarded as enticing to sin), [no matter how it comes or where it leads] has overtaken you and laid hold on you that is not common to man [that is, no temptation or trial has come to you that is beyond human resistance and that is not adjusted and adapted and belonging to human experience, and such as man can bear]." *I Corinthians 10:13a, Amplified Bible*

FROM HEAVEN'S STOREHOUSE

Oh, blessed Holy One,
You are my hiding place.
My refuge from the storms of life;
Protection by Your grace.

When overwhelmed, I rush to Thee,
My strength in time of need.
From shifting sand to solid rock,
You guide, You hear me plead!

From Heaven's storehouse You pour out
The treasures of Your love;
Great blessings and eternal peace,
Released from heaven above.

"But God is faithful [to His Word and to His compassionate nature], and He [can be trusted] not to let you be tempted and tried and assayed beyond your ability and strength of resistance and power to endure, but with the temptation He will [always] also provide the way out (the means of escape to a safe landing place), that you may be capable and strong, and powerful to bear up under it patiently."
I Corinthians 10:13b, Amplified Bible

"Don't worry about anything; instead, pray about everything. Tell God what you need, and thank Him for all He has done. Then you will experience God's peace, which exceeds anything we can understand. His peace will guard your hearts and minds as you live in Christ Jesus."

Philippians 4:6,7 NLT

"But let all those rejoice who put their trust in You; Let them ever shout for joy; because You defend them; Let those also who love Your Name be joyful in You. For You, O Lord, will bless the righteous; with favor You will surround him as with a shield." *Psalm 5:11,12*

HOW I LOVE YOU, HOLY JESUS

How I love You, holy Jesus,
How I praise Your holy Name.
From my heart I sing Your praises,
How I thank You that You came!

Came to earth to seek and save us,
Came to me, most needy one.
Filled my heart with Your great being;
In You all my battles won!

In the midst of each new battle,
Armed with all Your armor strong,
I stand firm on all Your promise;
Ready sword defeats each wrong.

How I love You, holy Jesus,
Blessed, only Potentate.
May I ever tell Your story,
Ruler of my life, my fate!

"Put on the whole armor of God, that you may be able to stand against the wiles of the devil…and take the helmet of salvation, and the sword of the Spirit, which is the Word of God." *Ephesians 6:11,17*

"For I know the plans I have for you", says the Lord. "They are plans for good and not for disaster, to give you a future and a hope."

Jeremiah 29:11 NLT

I'll Trust His Plan

God molds my life with steady hand,
That I may fit His holy plan.
He measures not by things of earth;
In Christ, His Son, God counts my worth.

I know not what each day will bring,
What trial of faith, what suffering.
Nor do I know what God will use
To deal this "self" its mortal bruise!

Though bitter cup of sorrow pour,
I'll walk by faith and trust Him more.
For Jesus holds my life secure;
What each day brings, I need not fear.

Though paths be clear or filled with haze,
I'll trust God more and sing His praise.
It's not for me to understand;
Instead, by faith, to trust His plan.

"Now faith is the assurance (the confirmation, the title deed) of the things [we] do not see and the conviction of their reality [faith perceiving as real fact what is not revealed to the senses]." *Hebrews 11:1 Amplified Bible*

"You will show me the path of life; in Your Presence is fullness of joy; at Your right hand are pleasures forevermore." *Psalm 16:11*

"The city had no need of the sun or of the moon to shine in it, for the glory of God illuminated it. The Lamb is its light." *Revelation 21:23*

God's Heaven-Land

Earth's mind can never comprehend
The beauty of God's Heaven-land;
Its purity, its radiant light,
Eternal joy, refined delight.

The absence of all sin and sorrow,
Always today and ne'er tomorrow.
A place of peace and righteousness,
All that is good, all blessedness.

All paths are filled with shining light,
With all things beautiful and bright.
Christ is the source of heaven's measure,
The Giver of its varied treasure.

We'll worship and adore Him there,
Our Shepherd and our Savior fair.
Our great High Priest, Redeemer-King;
Forevermore, His praise we'll sing!

"My thoughts are nothing like your thoughts", says the Lord. "And my ways are far beyond anything you could imagine. For just as the heavens are higher than the earth, so My ways are higher than your ways and My thoughts higher than your thoughts."

Isaiah 55: 8,9 NLT

"Yet in all these things we are more than conquerors through Him who loved us."
Romans 8:37

"He Himself has said, 'I will never leave You nor forsake you'." *Hebrews 13:5b*

KEPT BY HIS MIGHTY POWER

I commit my way to You, Lord,
And the way of all I hold dear,
Knowing You will guide and keep us,
Guard our hearts and abate our fear.

For You are our sun and shield, Lord,
All kept by Your mighty power.
In You, we are more than conquerors;
Our strength for each perilous hour.

As we fix all our thoughts on You, Lord,
Hiding Your truths within our heart,
Your word will never return void,
Nor from us You'll never depart!

"No one engaged in warfare entangles himself with the affairs of this life, that he may please Him who enlisted him as a soldier." *2 Timothy 2:4*

"But we all, with unveiled face, beholding as in a mirror the glory of the Lord, are being transformed into the same image from glory to glory, just as by the Spirit of the Lord." *2 Corinthians 3:18*

A WARRIOR FOR MY LORD

In my dreams of valiant splendor
I'm a warrior for my Lord,
Riding forth in clouds of battle,
Defeating devils with my sword.

Always faithful in the spirit,
Never changing in my quest,
To turn a soul to Jesus;
Ever giving Him my best.

But what heartbreak awaits my waking
As I look around and see,
That the person I'm becoming is not
Who I want to be.

I gaze into the mirror of my heart
And I behold,
Just a shapeless mass conforming
To this vain world's empty mold.

My Father, take this nothing,
With its vague outline of life,
Make me a warrior brave and fearless
For my Savior, Jesus Christ.

Send Your Spirit to infill me,
Let me heed your blessed call
When You say to me so softly,
"Not a part, I want your all."

I want no earthly praise to hear,
No medals on my breast,
But a crown of life in heaven
And to know His blessed rest.

To know I'll hear my Savior say
Through all eternity,
"Come sit with Me, beloved child,
For I am pleased with thee."

"For a day in Your courts is better than a thousand
[anywhere else]; I would rather be a doorkeeper
and stand at the threshold in the house of my
God, than to dwell [at ease] in the tents of the
wicked." *Psalm 84:10 Amplified Bible*

"Come to Me, all you who labor and are heavy-laden and overburdened, and I will cause you to rest. [I will ease, and relieve and refresh your souls]." *Matthew 11:28 Amplified Bible*

"He has put a new song in my mouth – Praise to our God; many will see it and fear, and will trust the Lord." *Psalm 40:3*

COME TO ME

Oh come to Me and drink
Of my deep and living waters.
Drink deeply from My source of love,
That heals your sons and daughters.

Oh come to Me and rest,
Where sin and sorrows cease to be,
Where singing fills the heart with joy,
Where powers of darkness flee!

Oh come to Me, beloved,
Come learn the songs I sing.
Forget the songs of grief and pain;
Rich joy My songs will bring.

Oh come to Me and pray,
For nothing is too hard for Me!
By faith believe My promises;
Great things I'll do for thee.

Oh come to Me and learn
I have a wondrous plan for all,
To fill each heart with songs of joy;
Oh hear Me as I call.

Oh come to Me receiving
The new song I'll give thee;
A song that's known to you alone,
A song You'll sing to Me!

What blessed hope and joy is ours when we refuse
the ways of thinking of our old nature and finite
understanding. Jesus longs to give us His precious
songs of love and peace, to gently whisper to our
struggling hearts…"Come to Me".

"Faith is the confidence that what we hope for will actually happen; it gives us assurance about things we cannot see...By faith we understand that the entire universe was formed at God's command, that what we now see did not come from anything that can be seen."

Hebrews 11: 1,3 NLT

FROM DEATH TO LIFE

Each day I seemed the more alone,
No one to heed my sobbing moan.
No one to comfort or to care;
My heart was weeping in despair.

I looked upon the world through tears,
My mind was filled with horrid fears!
I seemed to be alive, yet dead;
No rest to ease my aching head.

Eyes could not see but sorrow deep,
Feet did not move, but seemed to sleep.
Ears did not hear, but were o'er grown,
My tongue long silent, made of stone.

So tired was I, I laid me down,
But demons sought me like a hound!
Through miles of sleep I heard their roar,
To persecute me all the more!

Locked tight in time and bound by fear,
A day gone by seemed as a year.
Clocks did not move, but were so still;
My mind, a wound that would not heal.

Such loneliness I cannot tell,
I only know t'was surest hell!
Nor did I know from whence it came,
This prison dark, my mind to claim.

As I sat all alone one day,
A Stranger came along my way.
To my surprise he greeted me and said,
"Friend, may I sit with thee?"

He told me things I had not heard;
At first, they seemed to me absurd!
He talked of God who sent His Son,
Of greatest love, of victories won.

He said that in God's Son was life,
Who came to end in man all strife;
Who sought the souls of lonely men,
Of wretched ones so deep in sin.

My heart that I had thought long dead
Beheld the truth of what He said.
I knew that Jesus was the way;
He gave to me new life that day!

Such friendship I had never known!
My new Friend left me not alone,
But walked instead with me each day,
Explaining to me of God's way.

Of mysteries deep within God's word;
Such wondrous things I'd never heard!
From death to life and sweetest peace,
From darkest pit to life released!

This happened not so long ago,
This new life now in which I grow.
And like the One who rescued me
I seek to be a friend to thee.

To share with you my Friend so dear,
Who rescued me from all my fear.
This Friend is Christ, He is my all;
Come to Him now, He ever calls!

I was in Nursing School when I wrote this poem. We were in the Psychiatric quarter of school and had to go to the Psychiatric Hospital in Mt. Vernon, Alabama, to visit and work with the patients. It was so heart-breaking! How I wished that these poor people could know the Christ I loved. How I longed for them to know the One who alone could set them free. From that experience, the above poem evolved, based on Luke 5:1-20 where Jesus heals the demon-possessed man.

"Trust in the Lord with all your heart; do not depend on your own understanding. Seek His will in all you do, and He will show you which path to take. Don't be impressed with your own wisdom. Instead, fear the Lord and turn away from evil."

Proverbs 3:5-7 NLT

"Trust in the Lord with all your heart, and lean not on your own understanding; in all your ways acknowledge Him, and He shall direct your paths." *Proverbs 3:5,6*

WILL WE TRUST?

Will we trust He is the Christ
When sorrows crowd our hearts with tears?
Will we trust He is the Christ
When markets fail and bring us fears?

Will we trust He is the Christ
When leaders turn from His dear face?
Will we trust He is the Christ
When loved ones spurn His loving grace?

Will we trust He is the Christ
Who understands our every care?
Will we trust He is the Christ
And intercede with Him in prayer?

Will we trust He is the Christ
When persecution looms ahead?
Will we trust He is the Christ
And stand up strong for Him instead?

Will we trust He is the Christ
Who goes before us every day?
Will we trust He is the Christ
When Satan struts and brings dismay?

Will we trust He is the Christ
And will lead us where to walk?
Will we trust He is the Christ
And confess Him by our talk?

Will we trust He is the Christ
When each day grows darker still?
Will we trust He is the Christ,
Obey His words and trust His will?

Yes! We'll trust He is the Christ,
That He alone brings victory!
Yes! We'll trust He is the Christ,
For His dear face we soon shall see!

"Anytime we face an issue that we know is truly important, we need to go to the Word of God to find out what God says on the matter...The Bible is God's viewpoint; it is His opinion, His counsel and His advice...God's commandments, statutes, precepts, and principles cover all of life's situations. We need to ponder God's word – read it, study it, memorize it, think about it, and consider it. In doing so, we discover the wise way to handle life and to respond to the difficult situations we all face."

<u>God's Way Day By Day</u>[1]
Charles Stanley

[1] Charles Stanley, *God's Way Day By Day.* Thomas Nelson Publishers, Nashville, TN. 2007.

"Blessed are those who hunger and thirst for righteousness, For they shall be filled." *Matthew 5:6*

SEED OF FAITH

Dear Father, as a little child
I bring to You my need,
And cast my faith before You
As a tiny little seed.

In Jesus' righteousness alone,
I kneel before Your throne.
Your Holy Spirit fills my heart;
Assures me I'm Your own.

At times, I long for heaven so,
I feel my heart near bursts!
I reach out to You, Father,
With a never-ending thirst.

As I reach out my emptiness
You fill me with Your love,
And make me fit for life on earth
With glory from above!

This revelation of Yourself
The Holy Spirit brings,
And from that tiny seed of faith
New life and hope e'er springs!

"The apostles said to the Lord, 'Increase our faith…' and the Lord answered, If you had faith (trust and confidence in God) even [so small] like a grain of mustard seed, you could say to this mulberry tree, 'Be pulled up by the roots, and be planted in the sea', and it would obey you."

Luke 17:5a,6 Amplified Bible

"Therefore, as the elect of God, holy and beloved, put on tender mercies, kindness, humility, meekness, long-suffering;…But above all these things, put on love, which is the bond of perfection." *Colossians 3:12,14*

BLESS THIS FRIEND

Dear Lord, I've a friend that I love so dear
And one who loves You, too.
A silvery-haired friend, with a figure so bent,
Yet a spirit so straight and true.

Though pain is her lot, her time is not spent
In pity and grief for this cross,
But onward and upward the victory You give
And her cross is a gain, not a loss!

If, for a while, dear Lord I pray,
The pain of my friend I could bear,
Then perhaps she would know the depth of my love
For You and for her that I bear.

Each time that we meet there's a smile on her face,
So gentle, so kind and so true.
It lights up her soul and lifts up my heart,
Reminding me, savior, of You.

The aura of love that envelopes her face
Has a radiance so sublime.
I know it must come from time spent at Your feet,
For, dear Lord, it is so divine!

Whenever I think of this dear, precious friend,
I find my thoughts turning to You.
And whenever I see her I remember anew,
The love that you bear for me, too.

Words can't describe this rare friend of mine,
So Christ-like in every way,
So warm and so thoughtful; dear Lord I pray,
Bless this friend whom I love today!

From 1958 until 1972, we were members of Westlawn Baptist Church in Mobile, Alabama. I became close friends with our elderly custodians, the Merediths. On many Wednesday nights, I would visit Mrs. Meredith in their apartment, located in the back of the chapel.

Mrs. Meredith had Parkinson's Disease and was confined much of the time. She wrote beautiful poetry, and with my love for poetry, this became a strong tie between us. How I loved this dear lovely friend and this poem was written for her.

"And the ransomed of the Lord shall return, and come to Zion with singing, with everlasting joy on their heads. They shall obtain joy and gladness, and sorrow and sighing shall flee away." *Isaiah 35:10*

Bells of Heaven

Bells of heaven, songs of angels,
Bid the soul to worship Christ.
In Him all our sorrows gladdened,
Blessed King who gives us life.

In the blackness of earth's darkness,
Many times it's hard to hear,
God's sweet calling through the bell sound
Bringing Light, the Christ so dear.

Such a clear sound, sweet and pure sound,
As it fills the listening heart,
Overcoming sin's dominion,
Commanding demons to depart.

Listen, listen, eager pilgrim,
For the blessing of the bell sound,
Ringing out Love's sweetest message,
"Victory in Christ is found!"

In the battles of the thought-life
Lurk the giants of fear and pain.
Yet, with heaven's bells clear ringing,
Mighty foes for'er are slain!

Wise the heart that heeds the bell sound,
Hears the voice of God therein,
Rippling through the fiercest battles,
Freeing souls so bound in sin.

Then, amidst the tear-flow singing,
Thorn in hand or in the heart,
Peal the bells of heaven ringing,
"You are safe within the Ark!"

Sound of freedom on the hilltop,
As it rides the gentle breeze,
Sound of freedom in the valley,
As in Christ the heart believes.

Like the joyful songs of angels,
Is the voice of heaven's bells,
Filling saints with hope and gladness,
Casting sadness into hell!

Heaven's bells will ne'er stop ringing,
But each heart must will to hear,
God's great message of deliverance
In His Son, so very near.

Sounding through the tired earth singing,
Bells now ringing, bringing cheer,
Ever lingering in the heartland,
Love's infilling, Christ is here!

"As for me, I will see Your face in righteousness; I shall be satisfied when I awake in Your likeness."
Psalm 18:15

In His Image

My dear brother, my dear sister,
In your precious face I see,
Our Beloved, our dear Savior,
In whose image we're to be.

As our lives are fully yielded
To our God of love and grace,
Day by day our God will prune us;
From sin's likeness He'll erase.

Oh, to be like our dear Savior,
In our hearts and in our spirits,
Wanting only His desires;
Plead this prayer and God will hear it!

Day by day, He'll shape and mold us,
Purifying us as gold,
Until the day we wake in heaven
And His likeness to behold!

Oh, to be like Christ forever
In His Kingdom-land above;
Ever praising and beholding
Our great God of grace and love!

"We are assured and know that [God being a partner in their labor],all things work together and are [fitting into a plan] for good to and for those who love God and are called according to [His] design and purpose. For those whom He foreknew [all of whom He was aware and loved beforehand], He also destined from the beginning [foreordaining them] to be molded into the image of His Son [and share inwardly His likeness], that He might become the firstborn among many brethren."

Romans 8:28,29 Amplified Bible

"For our citizenship is in heaven, from which we also eagerly wait for the savior, the Lord Jesus Christ, who will transform our lowly body that it may be conformed to His glorious body, according to the working by which He is able even to subdue all things to Himself."

Philippians 3:20,21

"For to me, to live is Christ, and to die is gain."
Philippians 1:21

Roll On, Oh Years Unending

As I walk this life toward sunset
Life grows sweeter, deeper still;
For as years roll on unending
Jesus' presence does infill.

Jesus draws me closer to Him,
How His glory fills me so,
And I know He thinks about me
For the Spirit lets me know.

Though my steps may slow and falter
And my face may change with years,
In the Spirit I am singing,
For His second advent nears!

Oh, what joy to know His presence
And the fullness of His grace,
Just to know that on the morrow,
I'll see the sweetness of His face.

How I'll bask within His glory
In His kingdom – land of love,
Where I'll never, never wander
From that holy land above.

It's a new life He has given
When He died for you and me.
Lost and lonely? Come to Jesus,
Oh, what wonders you will see!

As I walk along His pathway,
In the light He sends my way,
I know my steps will never falter
For He gives the world no sway.

Love so brilliant, incandescent,
Shining bright, so crystal clear,
Blinds my eyes to all but Jesus,
Above all Whom I hold most dear.

Precious Jesus, Holy Saviour,
You're my cleft, my hiding place,
You're my feast, my banquet table,
You're my goal, the winning race!

So roll on, oh years unending,
For you have no fears for me.
Jesus holds my life secure,
Now and throughout eternity!

"Behold, I am coming quickly! Blessed is he who keeps the words of the prophesy of this book…amen. Even so, come, Lord Jesus!"

Revelation 22:7, 20b

BIBLIOGRAPHY

Carmichael, Amy. *Edges of His Ways.* CLC Publications, Fort
    Washington, PA. 1980.

God's Little Devontional Book for Moms. Honor Books, Colorado
    Springs, CO. 1995.

Stanley, Charles. *God's Way Day By Day.* Thomas Nelson Publishers,
    Nashville, TN. 2007.

"Christian love and help for the weak means humiliation of the strong before the weak, of the healthy before the suffering, of the mighty before the exploited."

- Dietrich Bonhoeffer

a place of grace.

OUR MISSION

To provide a safe residential environment to sexually exploited women, offering spiritual, mental, emotional, and physical support services. The WellHouse welcomes all women who have been sexually exploited and/or a victim of human trafficking. Regardless of race, color, creed, or religion, women in pain can be assured they will find love and acceptance in the arms of the WellHouse.

*A **victim** is a person who needs to be rescued.*
*A **survivor** is someone who has been rescued.*
*An **overcomer** is someone who has been healed.*

For more information please contact us at:

The WellHouse
8121 Parkway Drive
Leeds, AL 35094

www.the-wellhouse.org
Office: 1-800-991-9937
Crisis: 1-800--991-0948 (24/7)

FILL MY CUP, LORD[1]

Like the woman at the well I was seeking

For things that could not satisfy;

And then I heard my Savior speaking:

"Draw from My well that never shall run dry."

REFRAIN: Fill my cup, Lord, I lift it up, Lord!

Come and quench this thirsting of my soul;

Bread of heaven, feed me 'til I want no more-

Fill my cup, fill it up and make me whole!

There are millions in this world who are craving

The pleasure earthly things afford;

But none can match the wondrous treasure

That I find in Jesus Christ my Lord.

REFRAIN

So, my brother, if the things this world gave you

Leave hungers that won't pass away,

My blessed Lord will come and save you,

If you kneel to Him and humbly pray.

REFRAIN

[1] **FILL MY CUP, LORD,** Richard Blanchard
© 1959 Word Music, LLC All Rights Reserved. Used By Permission

About the Author

EMILY PERSONS McELHANEY lives in Birmingham, Alabama, with her husband of almost 59 years, Ken. They have three children, all married, eight grandchildren, three of whom are married, and six great-grandchildren. In 2013, Emily's left leg had to be amputated due to cancer. She testifies of God's faithfulness and uses her circumstances to witness to others. Emily has been a Bible teacher for over forty years and currently leads a Ladies' Bible Study in her neighborhood. Her passion is to inspire others to love God's Word, to spend time alone with Him and to discover God's unending love and special plan for their individual lives.

CPSIA information can be obtained
at www.ICGtesting.com
Printed in the USA
JSHW032031061020
8570JS00001B/2